# Albatrosses
## of Midway Island

# Albatrosses
## of Midway Island

by Sylvia A. Johnson
photographs by Frans Lanting

**A Carolrhoda Nature Watch Book**

Carolrhoda Books, Inc./Minneapolis

The author and publisher would like to thank Dr. G. Causey
Whittow, Professor and Chairman, Department of Physi-
ology, John A. Burns School of Medicine, University of
Hawaii at Manoa, for his assistance with this book.

The photographer would like to express his appreciation
to the U. S. Fish and Wildlife Service (Honolulu), the U. S.
Coast Guard (Honolulu), the U. S. Navy (Midway Island),
and also to ornithologists Harvey Fischer and Pete Prince
for their invaluable research on albatrosses.

LIBRARY OF CONGRESS CATALOGING-IN-PUBLICATION DATA

**Johnson, Sylvia A.**
    The albatrosses of Midway Island / by Sylvia A. Johnson ;
photographs by Frans Lanting.
        p.   cm.
    "A Carolrhoda nature watch book."
    Includes index.
    Summary: Describes the characteristics and activities of the
Laysan albatross which flies to Midway Island to breed. Also
discusses how birds and humans have learned to live together on this
small island in the Pacific Ocean.
    ISBN: 0-87614-391-5
    1. Laysan albatross—Midway Islands—Juvenile literature.
[1. Laysan albatross. 2. Albatrosses.] I. Lanting, Frans, Ill.
II. Title
QL696.P63J64   1990
598.4'2—dc20                                          89-32918
                                                       CIP
                                                       AC

Manufactured in the United States of America.

1  2  3  4  5  6  7  8  9  10  99  98  97  96  95  94  93  92  91  90

The bird soars on wide wings above the rough waters of the ocean. After swooping down until it almost hits the waves, it climbs again toward the sky. Rider on the wind, it goes for months without ever touching land.

This remarkable bird is an albatross. For centuries, people have seen albatrosses flying over the ocean, far from any land. In the past, sailors told stories about this mysterious creature of the open sea. Some thought that the albatross was a sign of bad luck. In other legends, the birds represented the souls of sailors who had drowned at sea.

Today, not many people believe these fantastic stories. But the truth about the albatross is almost as amazing as the legends of the past.

*A pair of Laysan albatrosses*

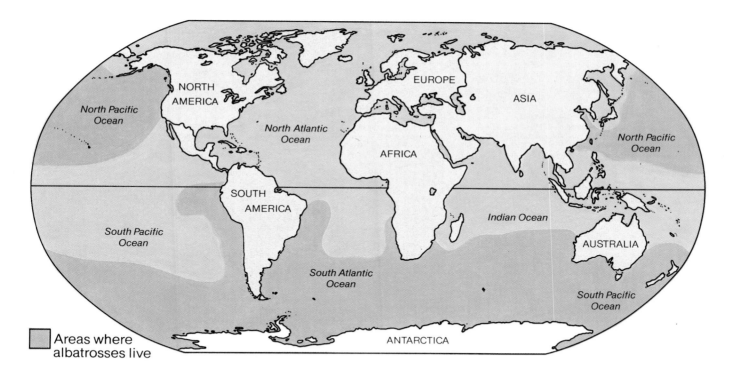

NORTH AMERICA
North Pacific Ocean
North Atlantic Ocean
SOUTH AMERICA
South Pacific Ocean
South Atlantic Ocean
EUROPE
ASIA
AFRICA
North Pacific Ocean
Indian Ocean
AUSTRALIA
South Pacific Ocean
ANTARCTICA

Areas where albatrosses live

The albatross family (Diomedeidae) includes the largest birds in the world. Some albatrosses have a wing span of at least 11 feet (3.4 meters). Others are not quite so large, with wings measuring 6 or 7 feet (1.8 or 2.1 meters) across. These amazing wings are only about 6 to 9 inches (15.2 to 22.9 centimeters) wide, very narrow compared to their length.

Regardless of their size, all albatrosses are graceful fliers. When the birds are on the ground, they are not always so impressive. They walk with a waddle and sometimes stumble over their big webbed feet. Because of their clumsiness on land, some albatrosses have been given the nickname **gooney birds.**

Most albatrosses are found flying over the oceans in the southern half of the world. They are common in the vast open seas between South America, Africa, and Australia. A few albatrosses live north of the Equator, soaring over the waters of the North Pacific Ocean. The pictures in this book show one of these northern birds, the Laysan (LAY-sahn) albatross. The scientific name of this species, or kind, of albatross is *Diomedea immutabilis.*

*Albatrosses soar on the wind when they fly. They hold their wings extended like the wings of a glider.*

Albatrosses live in both the northern and southern hemispheres, but the birds are not usually found in areas near the Equator. The winds are very light in these regions near the middle of the earth. Just like sailing ships, albatrosses don't do well in places where the wind doesn't blow.

In the areas north and south of the Equator, there are bands of strong **pre-vailing winds** that blow most of the time. Albatrosses depend on these winds to keep them moving.

When albatrosses fly, they ride on the wind. Unlike many kinds of birds, they do not need to flap their wings to keep themselves in motion. Instead, they soar on the moving air, holding their wings extended like the wings of a glider.

When an albatross is flying over the ocean, it often dives down close to the surface. Then it swoops up toward the sky. The bird will do this over and over as it moves along at speeds up to 70 miles (112.6 kilometers) per hour. This action allows it to take advantage of the movement of air over the water.

The air close to the surface of the water moves slower than the air at upper levels. As the albatross dives toward the waves, its body meets less resistance from the air. This causes the bird to move faster and faster.

Just before hitting the water, the albatross turns into the wind and begins to climb again. Like a roller coaster swooping up a hill, it uses the speed gained in its dive to give power to its climb.

Moving in this up-and-down style, an albatross can fly for thousands of miles. It seldom gets tired since it is using the energy of the wind to keep moving. Even in storms and gales, albatrosses can continue to soar over the sea.

*A Laysan albatross usually has a wing span of 6 or 7 feet (1.8 or 2.1 meters).*

*When an albatross comes in for a landing, it uses its big feet as brake flaps.*

There are only two things that cause albatrosses to stop flying. One is the need for food. An albatross gets its food at sea, and it lands on the surface of the water to eat.

To come in for a landing, the bird lifts its wings high and spreads its tail. As it approaches the water, it puts its big feet forward, using them as brake flaps.

Once an albatross is floating comfortably on the water, it is ready for a meal of its favorite foods, squid and fish. The birds often feed at night, when these animals can be found near the surface of the ocean.

Albatrosses get the moisture they need by drinking sea water. Their bodies need this salty water in order to function. The birds have special glands above their eyes that remove excess salt from their systems. The salty waste liquid produced by the glands comes out of their nostrils. It runs down grooves in their bills and drips off the ends.

After eating and drinking on the surface of the sea, an albatross is ready to fly again. It takes off by running along the water and flapping its wings. The wind eventually lifts the bird up, and it returns to its soaring flight.

*To take off from the sea, an albatross runs along the surface of the water.*

*When it is time to mate and have young, albatrosses return to land.*

The other thing that causes an albatross to leave the sky is the need to mate and reproduce. These important activities cannot be performed in the air or on the surface of the sea. They must take place on land.

12

While it is flying or feeding, each albatross usually stays by itself. When the time comes to mate and bear young, the birds get together with others of their kind. Like many sea birds, albatrosses form large groups known as **breeding colonies**. Each colony may be made up of thousands of birds.

Most albatross breeding colonies are located on islands in remote regions of the sea. At mating time, many Laysan albatrosses head for Laysan Island in the North Pacific Ocean. Others go to Midway, another island in the same area of the Pacific.

*A breeding colony of Laysan albatrosses on Midway Island*

13

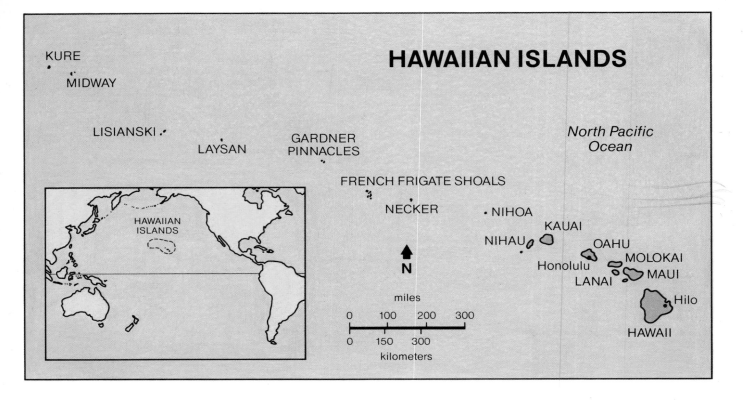

KURE
MIDWAY

**HAWAIIAN ISLANDS**

LISIANSKI
LAYSAN
GARDNER PINNACLES

*North Pacific Ocean*

FRENCH FRIGATE SHOALS

NECKER
• NIHOA

KAUAI
NIHAU
OAHU
Honolulu
MOLOKAI
LANAI
MAUI

Hilo

HAWAII

HAWAIIAN ISLANDS

N

miles
0    100    200    300

0    150    300
kilometers

Midway is actually made up of two small islands that are part of a circular **coral atoll** (A-tohl). It is located at the end of the Hawaiian Island chain, about 1,300 miles (about 2,092 kilometers) northwest of Honolulu. During World War II, an important sea battle between the United States and Japan took place near Midway Island.

Today, the U. S. Navy has a small base on Midway, but the island is better known for its colonies of albatrosses. Two species of the big sea birds nest on the island—the black-footed albatross

(*Diomedea nigripes*) and the Laysan albatross.

All the albatrosses that come to Midway for breeding are birds that were born on the island. No matter how far they have roamed, they come back to this speck of land to find mates and to have young.

An albatross spends the first few years of its life at sea. After leaving Midway as a youngster, it may never even touch land until it is at least three years old. Around this time, it is drawn by **instinct** back to the island of its birth.

14

*A Laysan albatross flies over a beach on Midway Island.*

When a young Laysan albatross makes its first return trip to Midway, it is ready to start the long process that will lead to mating and reproduction. Albatrosses mate for life, and they usually live for at least 30 years. It is not surprising that it takes them a long time to find just the right partners.

The first step in the process is to get acquainted with possible mates. When young Laysan albatrosses return to Midway, they form groups with other Laysan albatrosses of their own age. The birds spend most of their time together practicing the complicated **courtship dance** of their species.

15

16

Many kinds of birds and other animals go through a period of courtship before mating. They make special sounds and movements that attract males or females of their species. Through these courtship ceremonies, the animals find partners and get to know them before beginning the serious job of becoming parents.

Young Laysan albatrosses are born knowing how to perform the basic steps of their courtship dance. They know how to lift their wings, clap their bills, and make the different sounds used by all Laysan albatrosses. In order to do these things correctly, however, they need practice. Beginning around the age of three or four, the birds come to Midway for a few weeks each year to rehearse their "song and dance."

When a Laysan albatross is about seven years old, it is ready to begin courting in earnest. But first another important step must be taken. Each male albatross must find a piece of land, or **territory**, that is all his own.

*Bill-clapping is a part of the courtship dance of Laysan albatrosses.*

A male's territory only has to be big enough to hold a nest. But there is not much room on Midway Island. Often a male has to look a long time before finding a spot not claimed by another male. When he finally succeeds, the real courtship begins.

Standing on his territory, the male albatross performs to attract a female. He bows his head and makes a kind of whinnying sound. A female without a mate soon notices the courting male and comes to join him in the dance.

*A courting albatross does a wing-tuck while its partner watches.*

*At the end of their courtship dance, Laysan albatrosses point their bills at the sky and make a sound like "Mooooo." Scientists refer to this as a "sky-call."*

Facing each other, the two birds go through a complicated set of sounds and movements. They clap the two parts of their bills together. Sometimes the male or the female will do a wing-tuck, raising one wing high while ducking its head underneath. The dance usually ends with both birds standing on tiptoe, pointing their bills at the sky, and making a noise that sounds like "Mooooo."

19

*An albatross preening its mate's feathers*

After repeating their strange and beautiful dance many times, the two birds are ready to accept each other as mates. For a few weeks, they stay together on the male's territory. They sit side by side and **preen** each other's feathers. Sometimes they get up to dance or fly off to find food.

The albatrosses have formed a pair, but they are not yet ready to mate. The time that they spend together now will be a kind of "engagement" period. Mating will not take place until the following season.

Although the birds are not quite ready to mate and have young, they already know how to behave as parents. Included in that behavior is **incubation** (in-kew-BAY-shuhn), sitting on an egg to keep it warm. If the "engaged" albatrosses find some round object like a float from a fishing net, they may try to incubate it. In this way, they practice the skills they will need as parents.

*A pair of young albatrosses trying to incubate a float from a fishing net. When the birds are ready to breed, instinct may cause them to sit on any object that looks like an egg.*

After the engagement period, the two albatrosses separate and leave Midway to spend several months at sea. In October or November, they return to the island along with many other albatrosses that are ready to mate.

When they arrive, both birds go directly to the male's territory. There they greet each other excitedly and perform the courtship dance to renew the bond between them.

Now the proper time has finally come, and the two birds mate. The male's sperm cells enter the female's body and unite with an egg cell in her reproductive system. A baby albatross starts its development.

After going out to sea for food, the pair comes back to make a nest. The female does most of the work. First she forms a hollow in the sand with her body. Then she uses her feet to scrape out the hollow and make it deeper. With her bill, she makes a rim for the nest out of sand and plant material.

When the nest is finished, the female albatross lays a single egg in it. Soon after, she leaves to spend about three weeks at sea. Making the nest and laying the egg were big jobs. She needs food to restore her energy. Her mate will take care of the egg until she returns.

Unlike some other kinds of birds, a male and female albatross share in the incubation of their egg. An albatross egg must be incubated for two long months. During that time, the male and female take turns sitting on the egg. They nestle it against their **brood patch,** a featherless area of skin on the breast that keeps the egg warm.

*A Laysan albatross on its nest*

*Nesting albatrosses on a Midway beach wait patiently for their mates to return and take over the job of incubation.*

When the female returns to Midway after her weeks at sea, she takes over incubation from the male. By this time, he is very hungry and needs some food. The two birds go through a special ceremony when they change places. This is the way in which one partner lets the other know that the responsibility for the egg is being handed over.

Sometimes the exchange doesn't take place so smoothly. The bird sitting on the egg has become so attached to the job that it doesn't want to leave. Then its partner has to push and shove to get the sitter off the nest.

While each parent is at the nest, it spends some time "talking" to the egg. The adult brings its bill very close to the shell and makes a noise that sounds like "Eh...eh...eh." By doing this, the albatross parents teach their chick to recognize their voices even before it leaves the egg.

*This albatross has made a nest among some low-growing scaveola bushes. The red glow of sunset lights the sky behind the nesting bird.*

*An albatross egg begins to hatch.*

By February, the albatross eggs are ready to hatch. Like all birds, an albatross chick uses a special **egg tooth** on its bill to break out of its shell. First the chick makes a crack in the shell near one end of the egg. Then, turning slowly around inside the shell, it makes a whole row of cracks. Finally, it opens up a hole in the shell. To get out, the chick pushes from the inside until the end of the shell breaks off.

While the chick is hatching, the parent at the nest keeps a close eye on the process. The adult bird may encourage the chick by making noises, but it plays no role in helping the youngster to get out into the world.

Once their chick has hatched, the adult albatrosses still have a big job ahead of them. It will take about five months before the chick will be ready for life on its own. During most of this time, the parents will shelter the young bird, protect it, and provide it with food.

26

*This albatross chick is getting a meal of regurgitated food from one of its parents.*

For the first few weeks of its life, an albatross chick huddles in the nest, covered by the body of one of its parents. It is not yet able to control its own body temperature, so it still depends on its parents for warmth.

Just as during incubation, the parent birds take turns at the nest. While one bird is chick-sitting, the other is out at sea looking for food.

The adult albatrosses must often fly far out to sea to find squid and fish for themselves and their chick. Instead of carrying food back in their bills, as many land birds do, the adults bring it back inside their bodies.

The albatross parents feed their chick a mixture of partly digested food that they **regurgitate** (ree-GUHR-jih-tate), or bring up again, from their stomachs. Included in this mixture is a kind of oil produced in their stomachs especially for feeding the young bird.

*Even though this young albatross (right) is almost grown, it must still beg its parents for food. The young bird will not be able to get its own food until it has learned to fly.*

When a parent feeds the chick, the adult opens its large bill wide, and the baby puts its opened bill crosswise inside it. The stream of food passes neatly from the adult's mouth to the chick's.

After the first few weeks of a chick's life, the youngster needs so much food that both its parents must go out to find it. By this time, the chick is old enough to be left alone. It waits—sometimes not very patiently—for one of its parents to come back with food to fill its empty stomach.

On its nourishing seafood diet, the albatross chick grows rapidly. Its body soon becomes as round as a balloon. The chick will be fed by its parents until it is old enough to leave the island and find its own food.

When an albatross chick first hatches, it is covered with fuzzy grey down. In rainy weather, this downy coat often becomes soaking wet. Unlike the smooth feathers of an adult albatross, it does not shed water.

30

As a chick grows, its baby down is replaced by adult feathers. This change happens in stages. As a result, a chick often has patches of down on some parts of its body and sleek feathers on other parts. This combination makes the young birds look rather strange, as you can see in the photographs on this page.

*This chick is cooling itself by raising its big feet off the ground.*

By the time an albatross chick is several months old, it no longer spends all its time at the nest. It returns to the nest when its parents arrive with food because the adults will feed the youngster only at this spot. When it is not mealtime, however, the chick often wanders around the neighborhood. Sometimes it gets into quarrels with other young albatrosses that are also on their own.

When a chick is out in the sun on a hot day, it uses a special method to cool itself off. It sits back on its heels and raises the front of its large webbed feet. This position keeps the bird's feet off the hot ground and allows air to circulate around them. Every bit of cool air is welcome when you are stuck on a hot island without being able to fly away.

*As part of their flight training, young albatrosses get together to exercise their wings on the beach.*

The young albatrosses will not leave Midway Island until they are about five months old. By this time, they will have long wings like their parents. They will be able to glide on the wind to the far reaches of the Pacific.

In order to become expert fliers, however, the young birds will have to do a lot of practicing. First they must exercise their new wings so that they are strong enough to carry them over the sea. Sometimes large numbers of young albatrosses get together for an exercise session. They stand on a Midway beach and flap their wings vigorously.

33

*It takes a lot of hard work for an albatross to become airborne.*

Albatrosses learning to fly must also practice taking off and landing. These are the most difficult parts of albatross flight. It takes a long time for the youngsters to learn the correct methods.

While they are practicing on the beach and over the Midway **lagoon**, the young birds have all kinds of problems. With wings spread, they rise a few feet above the ground only to lose control and flop on their backs. When landing, they sometimes come down with a crash and tumble head over feet.

34

This learning period is a very dangerous time in an albatross's life. In addition to making crash landings on the beach, the birds often end up splashing into the lagoon. If they are unable to take off and become soaked with water, they may drown. As many as 10 percent of the young albatrosses born each year on Midway do not survive the period of flight training.

*This young bird got dunked in the Midway lagoon after an unsuccessful flight.*

For the young albatrosses that do survive, the day eventually comes when they are ready to make their first flights. This usually happens in July. Spreading their wings wide, the birds get a running start and soar into the air. They have become airborne creatures like their parents.

Once the young albatrosses have learned to fly, they will leave Midway and head out to sea. There is plenty of food in the sea, and the constant wind

*Spreading strong wings, a young albatross takes off for its first flight.*

*After it leaves Midway Island, the young bird will not return to land for several years.*

blowing over the waves will provide energy for their soaring flight. The young birds will not return to land for several years.

The adult albatrosses also leave the island in July. Their duties as parents are finished for this year. But they will be back on Midway in a few months' time, ready to begin again the cycle of courtship and reproduction.

*Albatrosses share the Midway beach with a large gun used to defend the island during World War II.*

For several months during each year, the small land area of Midway Island is occupied by thousands of albatrosses and other sea birds. The birds share the territory with a small number of people, who live on Midway year round.

Today, birds and humans exist peacefully together, but this was not always true.

During and after World War II, Midway Island was an important U.S. Navy airbase in the North Pacific Ocean.

Planes landed frequently at the Midway airport, and there were many service people living at the base. Soon problems began to develop between the humans and the gooney birds of Midway Island.

The major problem had to do with air traffic. Navy planes landing or taking off on the Midway runway frequently hit albatrosses that were also landing or taking off nearby. The birds were killed and the planes often seriously damaged.

The Navy decided that the Midway gooney birds had to go, but it didn't want to have them all killed. Instead, it tried various methods to make the birds leave on their own.

Thick smoke was blown over the albatross colony. Old truck tires were burned near the nesting birds. The albatrosses were blasted by the loud noise of bazookas and mortars being fired. But none of these efforts worked. The birds refused to be frightened away from the island or even to get up off their nests.

*It is very difficult to make albatrosses leave their eggs and nests. The U.S. Navy discovered this when it tried to frighten the birds off of Midway Island.*

*Even if they have to fly thousands of miles, young albatrosses find their way back to the island where they were born.*

The next step in the Navy's albatross campaign was to remove the birds from Midway. Adult albatrosses were loaded onto planes and flown to distant places in the North Pacific. Almost all the birds came back to their nests and young, some from thousands of miles away.

Then the Navy came up with another plan. If the adults could not be kept away from the island, maybe young gooney birds could be discouraged from making Midway their home.

To test this idea, reseachers took 2,000 young birds that were almost ready to fly and loaded them onto a barge. The barge was towed to an island 250 miles (402.3 kilometers) from Midway. After making their first flights from this island, perhaps the birds would return there when they were ready to breed. But the plan didn't work. Most of the young albatrosses eventually came back to Midway, the island of their birth.

These experiments demonstrated the albatrosses' remarkable ability to find their way home. But they did not get the birds off Midway Island.

After all their failures, the Navy finally gave up. It decided to try to live with the albatrosses instead of getting rid of them. First it came up with a way to avoid collisions between planes and birds. The area around the runway was leveled and paved so that albatrosses wouldn't make nests there. This helped to cut down on the number of accidents. The airplane traffic on the island was also reduced when the Midway base became less important during the 1960s and 1970s.

*Airplanes and albatrosses sometimes compete for landing space on Midway Island.*

*Hazards on the Midway golf course include wandering albatrosses.*

Other conflicts between albatrosses and humans were ended by a simple plan. The birds would be allowed to breed on Midway as they always had. The people on the island would learn to live with their feathered neighbors. And this is exactly what has happened.

Today, albatrosses share Midway Island with a few hundred people. The birds are everywhere. They make their nests on the lawns of offices and houses, on the golf course, and in the small cemetery. Chicks stroll along the island's roads and sometimes sit down in the middle to take a nap.

*It isn't easy to mow the lawn when it is covered with albatross nests.*

The people living on Midway have learned how to deal with the gooney birds. When driving, they wait patiently until wandering chicks cross the road. Sometimes they get out of their vehicles to move the birds gently out of the way. During the courtship season, they may go without sleep while albatrosses sing courtship songs under their windows.

It isn't easy sharing a small island with thousands of birds, but most people on Midway are willing to make the effort. They think that the albatrosses are worth it.

43

*Photographer Frans Lanting meets some Laysan albatrosses face to face.*

Because the albatrosses on Midway Island are protected, they are not afraid of people. It is possible to get very close to the adult birds while they are sitting on their nests. Young albatrosses also don't mind being observed. In fact, when young birds are practicing the courtship dance, they sometimes invite human observers to join them. They bow and moo to the people just as they would to other albatrosses.

Many researchers have come to Midway Island to study the Laysan albatrosses and the other seabirds that nest there. By watching the birds and photographing them, they have learned a great deal about their lives. This information has helped us to discover the remarkable truth behind the legends of the albatross.

44

# GLOSSARY

**breeding colonies:** groups of albatrosses and other seabirds that have come to land in order to mate and bear young

**brood patch:** an area of featherless skin on the breast of a bird that is incubating an egg. This patch of bare skin helps to transfer the heat of the parent bird's body to the egg.

**coral atoll:** a ring of coral surrounding an area of shallow water called a lagoon. As sand and soil build up on the coral, the atoll becomes a circular island.

**courtship dance:** a series of special movements performed by male and female animals in preparation for mating

**egg tooth:** a hard knob on a young bird's bill used in breaking out of the egg shell. After hatching, this special "tooth" falls off.

**gooney bird:** a nickname given to some albatrosses because of their clumsiness on land

**incubation:** the act of sitting on an egg to keep it warm

**instinct:** a pattern of behavior that is inherited rather than learned

**lagoon:** an area of shallow water inside a coral atoll. A lagoon is usually connected to the ocean by channels that cut through the atoll.

**preen:** to smooth and arrange feathers with the bill. A bird preens itself to keep its feathers in good shape. Birds preen each other as a means of communication.

**prevailing winds:** winds that usually blow from a certain direction. The circulation of air around the earth creates different bands of prevailing winds in the northern and southern hemispheres. There are no prevailing winds near the Equator.

**regurgitate:** to bring up again. Albatrosses and some other birds bring partly digested food up from their stomachs to feed their young.

**territory:** an area of land that one animal uses for breeding, hunting, or other purposes. Most animals will defend their territories against other members of their own species.

# INDEX

# ABOUT THIS BOOK

When photographer **Frans Lanting** was a child growing up in Holland, he was fascinated by albatrosses. After he became a wildlife photographer, he continued to be interested in these beautiful birds. A photo assignment on Midway Island in the 1980s gave him a chance to see albatrosses up close. He photographed the birds as they performed their courtship dance and raised their young, and he was impressed by their dignity and good manners. In addition to albatrosses, Frans Lanting has taken pictures of lemurs, penguins, monkeys, lions, and many other animals all over the world. His color photographs are often featured in such well-known magazines as *Ranger Rick, National Geographic,* and *International Wildlife.*

**Sylvia A. Johnson** is an author who has written about many fascinating animals. Her long list of books for young readers include such subjects as wolves, bats, hermit crabs, silkworms, and elephant seals. Of all the creatures she has studied, the graceful albatross is one of her favorites. An editor as well as a writer, Sylvia Johnson works at a publishing company, where she produces children's science books.